Foundations
of
Exchanged Life
Counseling

Richard F. Hall

The Publishing Ministry of
Exchanged Life Ministries • Englewood, Colorado

Published by:
Exchanged Life Ministries
7350 E. Progress Place, Suite 206
Englewood, Colorado 80111
(303) 770-5433
Order through:
The Life Bookstore:
E-mail: info@thelifebookstore.com
Web: www.thelifebookstore.com
(720) 248-7211

2nd Edition, October 1998

ISBN 978-0692827949
Printed in United States of America

Dedication

To Lavonne,
my wife,
who consistently, faithfully and unobtrusively
reminds me of a life centered on Jesus Christ

About the Author

Richard F. Hall has been directly engaged in the ministry of Exchanged Life Counseling since 1983. He has served as a member of Exchanged Life Ministries with responsibilities in counseling and education and as the director of the Exchanged Life Counseling Institute. This book has been written out of a growing concern for a clear, brief statement of the theory of Exchanged Life Counseling. It is the result of years of contemplation, research, and experience.

The educational background of Dr. Hall uniquely qualifies him to write this book. He has a diploma from the Prairie Bible Institute, a B.S. from the Philadelphia College of Bible, a M. Div. from the Denver Conservative Baptist Seminary, an M.A. from the Eastern Baptist Seminary and a D. Min. from Luther Rice Seminary. The emphasis of these studies has been Bible, Theology, and Personal Pastoral Ministry.

Professionally the author has been in the ministry full time since 1966. He has served as the pastor of three churches. He has also counseled and taught at the Philadelphia College of Bible and the Exchanged Life Counseling Institute, a division of Exchanged Life Ministries.

Contents

Introduction

Through the years of being engaged in a personal ministry to hurting people, I have noticed a lot of confusion about what is called Exchanged Life Counseling. This counseling is based on the message of the Bible that the Christian is united together with Christ. This message has been proclaimed down through the history of the Church.

The Scriptures teach that by the operation of the Holy Spirit each Christian, at the moment of salvation, is united together with Christ. This union is a union of life. The Christian continues to be unique in his own individuality and personal distinctiveness. At the same time the Christian is made inscrutably and indissolubly one with Christ, and so becomes a member and partaker of the community of saints of which Christ is the head.

In theological terminology, this union is designated as a "mystical union," because it goes beyond any earthly relationship in the intimacy of its nature, the transforming power of its influence, and the surpassing greatness of its consequences. Recognizing the wonder of this union, it could be defined as: that intimate, living, spiritual union between Christ and the believer, by virtue of which Christ becomes the focus of the believer's life (Phil. 1:21).

The application of this truth to a personal ministry or counseling framework was popularized by Charles R. Solomon in his book *Handbook to Happiness* published in 1971. Since then there have been many articles and books written on the subject. None of these has sought to set forth the theory of Exchanged Life Counseling. The sense for the need for such a book kept growing. I tried to encourage others to write something. As is so often the case, when a person sees a need, it is usually the Lord indicating that the person should do something about it. Therefore, this book is the result.

The purpose of the book is to set forth the basics of the theory of Exchanged Life Counseling. Each of the components of a counseling theory will be dealt with from the perspective of Exchanged Life Counseling.

Six questions are asked and answered, one for each chapter. These questions are basic for a counseling theory. What is the model of man you work from? What causes people to have problems? What qualifications must a counselor have? What method is followed? What techniques are commonly used? What is the goal of counseling?

Because this approach to counseling is distinctly Biblical, you will find considerable information dealing with theology. Added to the chapters giving the components of a counseling theory is a chapter on theology.

Hopefully, this book will be an informative and practical tool for those interested in learning about the theory of Exchanged Life Counseling and for those engaged in this ministry. Exchanged Life Counseling as set forth in this book is a Biblically-based, Christocentric, and client-focused approach.

8

Chapter One

A Working Model

The Lord God created mankind as a match-
less spiritual being having a unique personality and a distinctive physique.

A Working Model

Do you ever feel as if you are so confused that you want to spell confusion with a capital K? When trying to understand the makeup of man, confusion or rather Konfusion seems to reign. The purpose here is to set forth briefly the model of man that is used in Exchanged Life counseling. We will attempt to clarify certain terms that are often used indiscriminately. Hopefully, understanding of these terms will begin to clarify the makeup of man and eliminate some of the confusion that surrounds the subject.

The view of man's makeup that is taken will guide the application of God's Word to the problems people are facing. The model of man that is followed will lead to determining what is important and what is unimportant; what is central and what is peripheral; what is lasting and what is temporary.

Being clear about the model of a person's makeup will also help avoid wrong conclusions. Various passages of Scripture seem to indicate that people can live sinlessly in this life. Others can be seen as indicating that salvation brings no change in this life and is only forensic. The model of a person's makeup will greatly influence which, if either, of these ideas will be followed.

In Exchanged Life counseling, three important areas of life must be taken into account. first, is the physical area. This includes such aspects as speech, action and the five senses. Second is the psychological area. Such aspects as thinking, feeling and choosing would fall into this area. Third is the spiritual area. Here are such aspects as communion with God, worship of God, plus the residence of God the Holy Spirit within a person. To leave even one of these areas of life out of a basic model leaves gaping holes leading to a multitude of problems. Therefore, the model of man that is used in Exchanged Life counseling takes into account the three areas of life in which people function: the physical, the psychological, and the spiritual. (See Diagram 1.)

Before continuing to develop these three different areas of life, we will need to pause and consider how we use the term nature. Are people made up of one nature or two natures? There have been some very warm debates among believers about this subject. At times it has been dealt with so dogmatically that to differ would brand one as a heretic. Most of this heat has come from broad assumptions and partial information. By using specific definitions we will seek to avoid confusion and arguments.

Of the many definitions for the word nature, two fit the subject we are addressing. The most common definition we will call the primary or broad definition. This definition points out that nature is the special combination of a person's attributes which determine that a person is a human being. Attributes are the qualities or characteristics that can be ascribed to a person. This definition is used when making basic distinctions.

The less common definition we will call the secondary or narrow definition. This definition relates to the innate disposition of a person that affects the conduct. Disposition is the controlling mental or emotional qualities that determine a person's usual way of thinking or acting. This definition is used when referring to psychological functioning.

Keeping these two definitions separate can clarify many problems and cool some of the unnecessary heat that has been generated. When they are not understood, confusion and conflict can be the result. When only one definition is used and the other is left out, the conclusion could be that a Christian has two equal natures. One is good and one is evil. When both definitions are used the conclusion could be that the Christian has two natures that are not equal. One is primary essence and the other is psychological and expressive. (See Diagram 2.)

This can all read like a succession of words without a great deal of importance; but when you consider how it fits into Biblical teaching on the subject, you begin to realize how important the issue really is. To use only one definition, the primary one, could result in the position of a Christian being in Adam, a sinner, condemned and dead, while at the same time in Christ, a saint, justified and alive. The Scripture, however, will not allow both to be true at the same time. According to 1 Corinthians 15 and Colossians 3 the Christian was in Adam but now is in Christ. In Romans 5 and 2 Corinthians 5 the Christian is shown to have changed from being a sinner to being righteous. Also the Christian has changed from being dead to being alive according to Romans 5 and Ephesians 2. There is no such thing as an *Adam-Christ Christian*, or a *sinner-saint Christian*, or a *dead-alive Christian*. To teach this as true seems to the author to teach Taoism instead of Christianity. Taoism maintains that there is a constant conflict in the universe and the individual between yin and yang, light and dark, good and bad. This conflict is a conflict of equals. Christianity maintains that there is such a conflict, but that it is not between equals.

Confusion often comes from viewing experience as the determining factor instead of God's Word. We need to start with God's Word and use both the primary and secondary definitions. The previous references demonstrate that the primary nature of a Christian is in Christ, righteous and alive. There are also many passages that show that a Christian may act in agreement with that primary nature or in disagreement with it (1 Thessalonians 5; Hebrews 12 and 1 John 1). Thus a saint can sin; a person who is alive to God can act dead to God; one in Christ can behave as if still being in Adam. Actions may either show or deny what is really true about a Christian.

Keeping the two definitions of nature in mind, we need to return to and examine the three distinct aspects of a person's makeup before we can integrate them. There are the spiritual, the psychological and the physical aspects. Within these three aspects there are important distinctions. The spiritual and psychological are not material in substance; therefore, they cannot be evaluated by physical means. The body is material and can be physically evaluated.

Within the immaterial there are divisions between the spiritual and the psychological or personality. This difference can be illustrated by the temple as recorded in Hebrew 9:1-10. There were three areas: the Outer Court, the Holy Place and the Holy of Holies. The knowledge of these areas decreased as one moved from the outer to the inner. Any Jew could enter the Outer Court.

The priests alone could enter the Holy Place. Only the high priest could enter the Holy of Holies, and then only once a year. The divisions between the areas also changed. There was a stone solid wall around the Outer Court. The temple itself was a stone building, while there was a curtain between the holy place and the holy of holies. The further one moved inside the less was known and the less distinct the divisions became. (See Diagram 3.)

The Scriptural evidence that demonstrates that there is such a division between the personality and the spirit is sufficient enough to say that they are not the same. The evidence which follows moves from the weakest to the strongest. first, the statements of 1 Thessalonians 5:23 and Hebrews 4:12 seem to indicate that these two areas are not the same. Second, the account of the creation of man (Genesis 2:7 and Job 33:4) adds to this difference. God formed man's body and breathed into him a spirit and man became a living, i.e. psychological being.

The first two factors are not in themselves conclusive enough to determine a clear cut distinction between the spiritual and the psychological. Adding two more ideas to them is necessary. The third is the adjectival use of the word "psyche" which is translated as "life," "soul," or "psychological." Since there is no commonly used adjective for soul in English, the translators have used such words or phrases as "natural,""without the spirit," "unspiritual," and "sensual." You will find this adjective of soul which could be expressed "soulish" or "soulical" in the following passages: 1 Corinthians 2:14, 15:44, 46; James 3:15 and Jude 19. In each of these passages the adjective for soul is used in the original language. The last of these factors is the new covenant. The new covenant is stated in Isaiah 43, Jeremiah 31, Ezekiel 11 and 36. The most extensive account is in Ezekiel 36. In this passage the Lord speaks of giving a new heart and a new spirit while removing the old. He then goes on to add that His Spirit will also reside within the new human spirit. This passage is later applied to Christians in Hebrews 8 and 10.

The four factors we have examined point to the conclusion that man is a tri-unity composed of a spiritual part (the spirit) a psychological part (the soul) and a physical part (the body). The recognition of these distinctions is necessary in Exchanged Life counseling. When they are not recognized, confusion results.

Application of these distinctions shows how important they are. Change is one of the major objectives in any counseling, and in Exchanged Life counseling it is central. When change is brought to bear on the three distinct areas, the following results are seen. The spiritual area of life has already been changed through God making an exchange. The psychological area is being changed. This twofold change is shown in Hebrews 10. The physical area according to Romans 8 is still not changed but will be changed in the future. (See Diagram 4.)

Personal identity is another major issue where the threefold distinction is important. The way it applies is in the understanding of what God says is true about the identity of the Christian. The basic identity of the Christian is essentially spiritual. When one does not know Christ as his Savior he functions with a primary or essential identity that is psychological. At salvation the Lord brings about a major change so that the spirit is new (2 Corinthians 5:17). Self-identity must now come from the spirit instead of from the soul and body. (See Diagram 5.)

We need to summarize what has been presented. People function in three major areas of life: the spiritual, the psychological, and the physical. These are each distinct and different. The nature of a person must be considered in both a primary and a secondary way. The primary nature is the basic essence of who a person is and is spiritual. The secondary nature of a Christian is the way he normally thinks, feels and chooses to act and is the psychological functioning. Therefore, within the nonphysical the distinction between the spiritual and the psychological must be maintained. The spiritual is the real essence of who people are. The psychological (i.e. soulical) is an important part of a person and is to express the life of the spirit. The physical is the vehicle for the expression of this life in a physical world.

THREE INTERRELATED AREAS OF LIFE

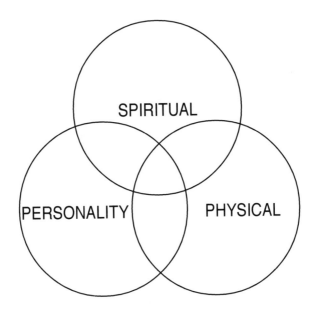

Diagram 1

NATURE OF A CHRISTIAN

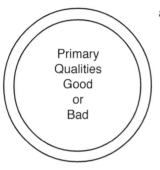

a. Using only the BROAD DEFINITION OF NATURE — good characteristics of a Christian, bad characteristics if not a Christian

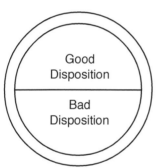

b. Using only the NARROW DEFINITION OF NATURE — for the Christian the disposition is both good and bad; for the non-Christian it is only bad

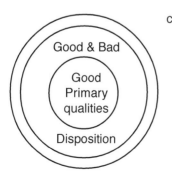

c. Using BOTH THE BROAD AND NARROW DEFINITION OF NATURE — for the Christian good characteristics while disposition is both good and bad; for the non-Christian it is only bad

Diagram 2

TEMPLE DIVISIONS

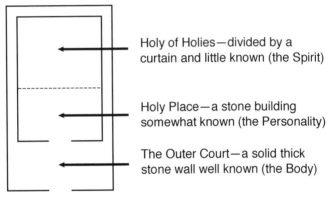

Holy of Holies—divided by a curtain and little known (the Spirit)

Holy Place—a stone building somewhat known (the Personality)

The Outer Court—a solid thick stone wall well known (the Body)

Diagram 3

Stylistically this could be drawn:

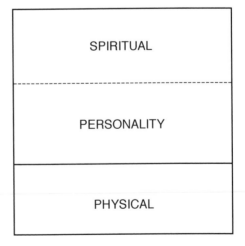

SPIRITUAL

PERSONALITY

PHYSICAL

Diagram 4

CHANGE HAS, IS, AND WILL TAKE PLACE

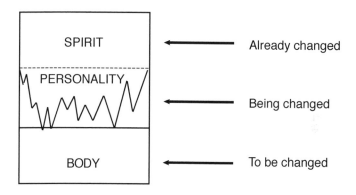

IDENTITY FOCUSED ON ONE AREA

Diagram 5

Chapter Two

The Causes of Problems

The Christian living life out of his or her own resources with or without seeking God's help is living a self-centered life that causes all kinds of problems.

The Causes of Problems

Because Scripture is the basis for Exchanged Life counseling, we must turn to it to find out what causes people to have problems. Philosophy sets forth causes of problems. Psychology sets forth other causes of problems. Sociology sets forth yet different causes of problems. When we study Scripture, we find that the causes people have pointed out are not the basic problems, but are symptoms of an even more foundational problem.

Genesis 3 records sin entering the human race. As a result there have been all kinds of difficulties that people have faced. Individuals who seek counseling may face problems that come from living in this world. Romans 8:18-25 reveals that his world is under the curse of sin. People, Christian or not, cannot live in this world without being affected by it. The entrance of sin is the major factor causing the problems people face in such areas as: physical, spiritual, financial, relational, emotional, and vocational.

The Christian faces the same set of circumstances as those who do not know the Lord. Because of the changes that have taken place at salvation, the Christian faces more causes for problems then those who do not know the Lord. The Christian is not in harmony with sinful society like the non-Christian is.

Many have maintained that the Christian faces more problems then the unsaved because of the "old man." The old man specifically defined is the unregenerate human spirit. According to Romans 6:6; Colossians 3:9, and other passages, at salvation the old man died, was removed and replaced with the new man. Therefore, the old man is not the cause of the problems that the Christian faces.

There are, along with sin, two other causes of problems for Christians. They are often paired together because of similarity. We will deal with them separately here for clarity. These two are indwelling sin and flesh. Indwelling sin is an inner temptation to sin which tempts us to think, feel, choose, and act sinfully. This is an ongoing problem for Christians because we are not yet glorified. Indwelling sin is in total agreement with the sinful world system in which all of us live. Paul spoke about indwelling sin in Romans 7:14-25 in a personal way to help us understand what it is that we are facing. Through indwelling sin believers cause problems for themselves through their sinful thinking, feeling, choosing, and acting.

Very closely aligned with indwelling sin is the flesh. Whereas indwelling sin is only referred to a few times, flesh is referred to 163 times in the New Testament and over 250 times in the Old Testament. We will focus on the New Testament usage. The word flesh has many different usages, such as: the skin of the body, people in general, ancestry, the world with its standards or just plain earthly. The most common usage of flesh is to point out the personality of an individual that is focused on self-centeredness.

The chief characteristic of flesh, self-centeredness, has been defined very well by Langdon Gilkey; "Self-centeredness is a loss of God at the center of the meaning and security of one's life, as the ground of one's trust and self confidence. Therefore, the self is left alone, autonomous, self-sufficient, insecure and anxious, fearful for itself, its future fame and glory. Placing itself in the center of its world, making itself, or its group, its god, and thence follows its bondage to defend itself and its security against all comers." (The source of this quote is unknown to the author.) This extensive description can be narrowed down to a precise definition: flesh is the condition of a person living life out of his or her own resources with or without seeking God's help to do so.

Flesh, which can be identified as a major cause of the problems Christians face, is not a division of man's makeup or a substance within but a condition of the personality living in agreement with sin. This condition is a carry over from pre-conversion days consisting of habits, emotions, ideas and memories of how to live life. The society that we live in does not depend upon the Lord; therefore, it constantly gives input which teaches and affirms a way of living that is only according to human resources. Simply stated, flesh is our independent self-centered way of living.

The above definition shows how the fleshly living patterns create real problems for Christians. The same patterns of living cause problems for non-Christians because they are ineffective; yet they are not as great as for Christians. The non Christian is spiritually in agreement with sin, but this is not true of the Christian.

A good example of the ineffectiveness and sinfulness of fleshly living patterns is given by Jeremiah the prophet. In chapter two, the Lord speaks about His people forsaking Him and at the same time seeking their own ways to satisfy themselves. The Lord calls these ways "cisterns that are broken and cannot hold water." They don't work; therefore, they don't satisfy.

Why do people follow such patterns of living if they are sinful and ineffective? One of the reasons is the habit of always seeking to live life in their own resources. Ever since the fall of man recorded in Genesis 3, independence rather than dependence on the Lord has been a characteristic of mankind. Christians, even though recognizing the impossibility of self-salvation, often seek to live for the Lord in self-effort. Another reason is the drive to avoid hurt while seeking to meet needs by using previously learned methods. These methods (i.e. fleshly living patterns) may only be 10 percent effective, but they seem to be better than nothing. Many of God's people have a false view of who they are, and they live according to that view. When one does not know who he is according to God's truth, he will live after the fleshly living patterns he has learned. The basis for understanding who we are is either God's evaluation or man's insights.

What are fleshly living patterns like? To list all of the ways Christians can live after the flesh would take many pages. We will consider here some of the more prominent ways. Romans 8:5-8 points to having the mind set on what the flesh desires which results in rebellion against God. Galatians 5:19-21 lists such fleshly living patterns as: sexual immorality, impurity, debauchery, idolatry, witchcraft, hatred, discord, jealousy, fits of rage, selfish ambition, dissension, factions, envy, drunkenness and orgies. We might want to list these kinds of activities in various categories, such as not so bad, bad, and really bad. Regardless, the Lord puts them all together as fleshly living patterns.

People face problems. In Exchanged Life counseling, the cause of those problems is threefold. The first is the entrance of sin and the resulting curse. This accounts for organically caused problems that need a physician's attention. This also causes great spiritual need which is where the Exchanged Life counselor starts by sharing the gospel. Spiritual need is man's greatest deficit. The second is the power of indwelling sin which militates against God. The third is the major one in Scripture for Christians and consists of fleshly living patterns which are always self-centered.

With this threefold foundation of the causes of people's problems, the Exchanged Life counselor has a framework to understand what is taking place. Helping people learn the difference between a self-centered life and a Christ-centered life must be done with clarity. Understanding the causes of the problem being faced will not in itself bring about change. Such understanding is a great advantage in seeing the need for change and leading the Christian to cry out with Paul, "Who shall deliver me...?" The only answer is Christ as Savior, Lord and Life.

Chapter Three

Counselor Qualifications

An Exchanged Life counselor must be qualified to guide people in spiritual growth and not be an information-giver telling what should be done.

Counselor Qualifications

Often when an individual is introduced, his work and credentials are given. Business cards normally list various important qualifications along with the name of the person. Look over the pages of counselors listed in the yellow pages and you will find such notations as Susie Q. Helper, Ph.D., Licensed; John Q. Helper, M.S.W., L.S.W. & A.C.S.W., Susie Q. Helper, L.C.S.W., C.A.C. III, or John Q. Helper, M.A., Licensed Counselor, Clinical Member A.A.M.F.T. These kind of notations are used to give credibility to the individual listed. We live in a society and time when many people–if not most– look for degrees, certification and license. Do such things guarantee credibility? Maybe. Maybe not.

There are many people that are hurting and are seeking someone to help them with their hurts. A major problem is that there are unscrupulous people who are ready to prey on these hurting people for their own personal benefit. Because there are no government licensing procedures for religious counseling, some of these people will set themselves up as Religious or Christian counselors. The purpose of some for using such terms may not be that they are Christian in their methods, but that they want to avoid any scrutiny by anyone else and the arduous, time consuming preparation usually required to be a counselor.

Not everyone can be a counselor. Just because a person wants to help others is not in itself an indicator that he is able to do so. Two questions about qualifications will guide us in demonstrating this. Why should a counselor have to be qualified? What are the qualifications that must be met to be a counselor?

To answer the first question, there are two very good reasons why a counselor should be qualified to be a counselor. The first is to protect the client. There are, as we have noted, unscrupulous people who only cause more hurt for people who are already hurting. There are some real horror stories about the way some unqualified counselors have damaged their clients. By requiring qualifications it is hoped that this kind of thing can be prevented or at least reduced. There are also those who are well meaning. Their hearts are in the right place. They would never purposely seek to hurt another person, but they are uninformed.

Being uninformed this kind of counselor can arrive at conclusions and guide clients in erroneous ways that are at best meaningless and possibly even detrimental. To protect the client, the counselor should be trained to be a counselor.

Another reason why a counselor should be qualified is to protect himself. There are people who are skilled in using other people. Such people can manipulate an unqualified counselor for their own ends, and the counselor will not be aware of it. The counselor also needs to protect himself from assuming too much concerning his own ability. For instance, a counselor who is unqualified can believe that he is skilled and able to be of total help in every area because he does not realize his own limitations. The counselor also needs to protect himself from becoming a rescuer, thus taking responsibility for the client's life from the client.

Noting these reasons as to why a counselor should be qualified to be one, the second major question that needs to be asked is, what are these qualifications that should be met? The qualifications we will consider fall into two categories: personal and training.

Because Exchanged Life counseling focuses on the spiritual area of life, this area has very definite personal spiritual requirements. The first of these spiritual requirements is salvation. Without a personal experiential reality of salvation it is impossible to be of spiritual assistance. In fact, everything in Exchanged Life counseling is based upon a personal experiential knowledge of Christ as Savior. Being born into God's family by faith in the shed blood of Christ does not alone meet all of the spiritual qualifications; there is also the need for brokenness and a total surrender to the absolute lordship of Christ in every area of life. The unbroken, unsurrendered Christian is not able to engage in Exchanged Life counseling. finally, the truth of Christ-centered living needs to be a regular part of life not just an idea that is only known about. The Exchanged Life counselor must be living the reality of his identification with Christ. This is because the counselor is not a direction-giver dispensing truth from an information booth, but a wilderness guide down paths he already has traveled himself.

Along with the spiritual qualifications are the psychological ones. The counselor's life should be a balanced one that demonstrates maturity. For the clients, the relationship with the counselor may be the only mature relationship that they have. The counselor who is qualified and effective is one that continues to grow. Learning about people, learning the Bible and relating them to each other never ends. Empathy, acceptance, concern and other emotional aspects can't be static but need to be constantly honed and expanded.

The third area of personal qualifications is the physical area. The practice of self-control to maintain good health is expected. It is extremely difficult to counsel people when the physical presence of the counselor communicates no control. This is not to say that an individual with physical limitations and health problems is unable to counsel. But the general pattern should be one of maintaining good health.

The other major category of qualifications is that of training. What kind of training is necessary for an Exchanged Life counselor? Because the counseling is focused on the spiritual aspects, the academic training can be minimal or extensive. There is a temptation to focus on either end of this spectrum. The focus here will be in the middle while recognizing that there can be advantages on either end.

Two areas of academic training stand out as most important. To minister to the spiritual aspect of life a good overall grasp of Scripture is invaluable. This can best be obtained from a Bible college or seminary. It can also be obtained by extensive careful personal study. To understand those individuals being ministered to is also needed. This can be learned by the study of psychology in a college or university. It can also be learned by being an astute observer of people in the many situations of life.

Professionally, the Exchanged Life counselor needs training in communication skills. The nature of counseling brings out the ability of the counselor to communicate or not communicate. These skills can be learned. The better they are known the better the counselor can understand and aid the client. If at all possible the Exchanged Life counselor should not be a "lone-ranger." It is too easy to get off center and not realize it when working all alone. Therefore, if at all possible, some arrangement should be made for association and/or supervision. Accountability when dealing with highly complex people and situations goes a long way toward preventing mistakes which hurt instead of help people.

The Exchanged Life counselor counsels from God's Word. Therefore, one of the fundamental requirements for leadership in ministry–not a novice–is also key in this ministry. In fact, almost the whole list of requirements given in I Timothy and Titus for leadership in the church would be excellent requirements for an Exchanged Life counselor. What we are specifically looking at here is experience; experience in knowing the Lord, experience in living the Exchanged Life, experience in seeing the changeableness of life, experience in ministering God's Word to people and experience in counseling skills. This is needed because the Exchanged Life counselor is a personal guide not a direction-giver. Counseling is from life not from a text book. Such counseling can only come from being experienced in the areas referred to previously. How can such counseling experience be obtained? The best way is by working with and under one who is already counseling.

Does this mean that the Exchanged Life counselor must have experience in all areas of life in order to be able to help? Generally not. But it is necessary to be spiritually mature. The Lord is responsible for the client's life not the counselor. From personal experience with the Lord the counselor can guide the client to the Lord's resources that are totally sufficient.

If a person meets all of the qualifications that have been set forth, would he then be a good Exchanged Life counselor? Because of the nature of life the answer is maybe. There are those individuals who have all the training and qualifications necessary but may not be good counselors; however, these qualifications are a great aid. They are usually a good indicator of one who is a good counselor.

Should these qualifications be required? The personal qualifications must be absolutely required, and usually the training qualifications are necessary. Because Exchanged Life counseling is religious counseling some people are drawn to it just to avoid the requirements of secular counseling. They want to be counselors and want to avoid a lot of hard work to qualify. In Exchanged Life counseling, there are strenuous qualifications that are required, particularly in personal areas. Obviously, therefore, a person should not seek to become an Exchanged Life counselor in order to avoid meeting qualifications.

Chapter Four

A Method of Ministering

There is a clear method used in Exchanged Life counseling that provides a way to deal with people's problems and bring about change, but the method must be adapted to the client in need.

A Method of Ministering

When the Exchanged Life counselor seeks to help hurting clients, the makeup of people and the causes of people's problems are always in the background. As has been previously pointed out, people are threefold in their basic make up: spiritual, psychological, soulical and physical. Salvation has already caused a spiritual change which starts a progressive psychological or soulical change and guarantees a future physical change. The multitude of problems people face began with the entrance of sin at the fall. Therefore, people are now faced with a world system that is opposed to the Lord, indwelling sin that pushes away from God and fleshly living patterns that lead to independent living. These factors greatly influence the way we must minister to people.

Exchanged Life counseling is not just a free-flowing general conversation between a counselor and a client. It is not a one shot, quick fix, i.e. "pray this prayer and your problem is solved," type of counseling. It does not include a rigid "cookie cutter" formula that every counselor and client must fit into. It definitely is not shrouded in a mystery which can only be understood and used by a select few of super counselor saints. To clarify some of the misconceptions that can arise, we will examine the process of Exchanged Life counseling. In so doing we will be showing how this method of counseling enables change to take place.

When first meeting with a person seeking help, the counselor must bring into play all of the communication skills at his disposal to analyze the client. Assessment involves several aspects. To begin with the counselor seeks to assess the client's problem. The counselor must seek to understand as fully as possible what is taking place in the client's life. This aspect of assessment should not be overemphasized or under-emphasized. To under-emphasize it would communicate a lack of compassion for the client. To overemphasize it would lead to the client's focus on this problem as being the only one. Usually the presenting problem the client is facing is evidence of a deeper issue

While learning what problem the client is facing, the counselor needs to also evaluate his ability to help. The counselor who thinks he can help everyone regardless of the nature of the problem is sadly mistaken. For example, take a person who is facing an organic problem. A physician is needed to deal with the physically based difficulties; nevertheless, an Exchanged Life counselor might help a person accept and be at peace with certain medical procedures or physical impairments.

The Exchanged Life counselor may also use various instruments to aid in his assessment. The type of instrument used would depend on the academic and professional background of the counselor. One instrument that can be used by nearly anyone is the Biblical Personal Profile. Because this instrument is designed to be self administered and self-interpreted, there are no requirements that must be met for its use. This Profile is a helpful tool for people to begin to understand behavioral tendencies. It is also useful for the counselor to begin to understand the counselee.

After beginning to understand something of what the client is facing and what is being done about it, the counselor needs to take a personal history. The past is the past and can't be changed, so why should we look into it? Did not Paul say in Philippians 3 that we should forget what is in the past? These are good questions. Why spend time on the life story of the client? There are two very good reasons. The first is to get to know this individual. The client comes as a stranger with a complex view of life totally unknown by the counselor. Taking a personal history aids in getting to know what this person has been through.

The second reason is to begin to see the patterns that have developed in the ways that the client deals with life. Because these methods often become self- centered patterns for living, they can be called fleshly living patterns. By spending time understanding what has taken place in a client's life and how he has chosen to respond to various circumstances, it is possible to detect some of the ways that have been developed to deal with these circumstances.

The third reason for taking a personal history is to learn how God's Word can be personally applied. Assignments to be completed between counseling sessions and the use of Biblical material during the sessions must always be applicable to the client's life. General, abstract or theoretical usage of Scripture means very little to the individual who is hurting. By taking time to get to know the individual, the counselor will be able to relate the Scripture to the client and the client's situation in a very personal way that is clearly understood by the client to fit his life.

There are several methods that can be used to enable us to know another person. The simplest to use and remember is the use of a chronological pattern. The counselor knows what has been covered and what needs to be covered. The client also knows where we are and is not lost in the process. When spending this time on taking a personal history, the counselor should not be locked into a definite chronological time structure, but should be free to move out of it if necessary. It can be returned to after a special subject has been covered. The time needed to learn about a person's life varies with each person. There is no set amount of time that should be followed. It depends on what has been taking place and the client's ability to relate that information.

To learn about a person's life without utilizing the information is not helpful to the counseling process. After obtaining a personal history, the Exchanged Life counselor should seek with the client's help to integrate the past with the present.

The process that can be used is to select significant major events
that have taken place in the client's life and determine the feelings that have resulted. Both the events and the feelings usually lead the client to basic assumptions and beliefs about himself and life. Using this thinking, feeling and beliefs, he has
developed his own living methods to seek to get his needs met
while at the same time avoiding being hurt.

Many different kinds of living methods can be developed, all of which come from the personal history. The result
will be that the client begins to understand why he feels, thinks,
and acts in the present circumstances the way he does, and
why it is ineffective. In most of this process the client usually
does not bring the Lord into the picture. By showing that God
created us with basic needs which only He can meet, the client
is made aware of the ineffectiveness he demonstrates in meeting his needs. These methods of dealing with life out of one's
own resources can be called fleshly living patterns or as 1 John
5 puts it, " idols." The Amplified Version expands the term
idols clearly pointing out that idols can be "anything and everything that would occupy the place in your heart due to God,
.... any sort of substitute for Him that would take first place in
your life." (See Diagram 6.)

After pulling together a client's life story and showing
why life isn't satisfactory, the need for change becomes evident. The first step in Exchanged Life counseling to lead to
change is to show how that change can take place. This must
be done in a very personal way, relating truth constantly to the
client in light of the present situation. We have already noted
that Exchanged Life counseling is not primarily used to ad-
dress organically based problems. The spiritual and psychological areas are where the focus is when the personal history
is obtained and analyzed. Where does change come from? The
power for change does not come from the counselor, nor from
the client (Jeremiah 13:23). Power for change comes only from
the Lord. The counselor will then need to point the client to
God's truth about what took place at salvation and how it applies to what is happening at present. Exchanged Life counsel-

ing seeks to teach the client the truth of his new identity, i.e., a Christian identity instead of an Adamic identity. There is a primary need to review what Christ has done for the client. Such passages as Romans 3 and 5, Ephesians 1 and Hebrews 9, along with many others show that Christ shed His blood for mankind's redemption. If the client is not a Christian, this is a good time to stop and share the gospel. Salvation is the beginning of the spiritual means for change. Without the reality of salvation Exchanged Life counseling is of no value.

The second step is to point out the client's former identity. All people before salvation are identified with Adam. That is their natural identity out of which they live. Because of being identified with Adam, Romans 5 teaches that the following are true: spiritual death, condemnation and sinfulness. No wonder the non-Christian faces problems; and, similarly, a Christian living as a non-Christian in Adam faces even more problems.

The third step is to share with the client God's truth about his identity in Christ since he has become a Christian. The counselor needs to emphasize not only what the Lord has done *for* the client but also what the Lord has done *in* the client. Romans 6, Ephesians 4 and Colossians 3 show that the old man is dead. A change has taken place spiritually. The old man has been replaced by the new man (2 Corinthians 5). The client is shown that he is identified with Christ in His death, burial, resurrection, ascension and seating in the heavenlies (Galatians 2 and Ephesians 2). In Christ the Christian is spiritually alive, justified and righteous. (See Diagram 7.)

All of this knowledge can be just information to write into a notebook and forget. That is why the Exchanged Life counselor must relate to the client this information, and seek to help the client to appropriate this truth for himself. Without that personal appropriation the client will leave the truth of God outside of his life and not see its relevance. This point of "crossing the line" or appropriation can be an easy step or it can be a traumatic change. It often involves the brokenness of a self-centered life so it may be exchanged for a Christ-centered life. That is where the term Exchanged Life counseling originated.

The client needs to come to the end of his own resources. He cannot of himself meet his needs nor avoid being hurt. His best effort will always fall short. The counselor should lovingly walk with the client through this very important area. Without resolution the client will continue living in his own way and be in bondage to the same problem with which he came. Most people want to change the people around them or the circumstances, but neither will provide lasting results. God seeks to change the person and brokenness is usually the first step.

Is this personal appropriation a quick conclusion to the problems hurting people face? No! It is the beginning of a process. The client is now cooperating with the Lord instead of fighting against Him. Changes may be swift and dramatic or they can be slow and deliberate. The temptation is to assume everything will be different immediately. The Lord reveals His life in us in ways that are unique to the individual. The character of the Christian is to become more and more Christ-like. Such character in a Christian is completely reached only when the Lord returns or when the Christian goes to be with Him, not before.

There is a clear method used in Exchanged Life counseling that provides a way to deal with people's problems and bring about change. What has been written here can be summarized in six steps.

First, the Exchanged Life counselor must assess the problem the client is facing, the client, and his own skills to determine if he can be of help.

Second, the social history of the client needs to be learned, being alert to the patterns of living that have developed.

Third, what has been learned about the present problem and the past living patterns needs to be brought together for the client, so has to reveal why the problem is there and why change is needed.

Fourth, the power for change for the Christian through his identification with Christ in death, burial, resurrection and seating in the heavenlies is taught methodically and personally. Fifth, after examining what has taken place and what God affirms to be true, the client is led to appropriate the truth of his identity in Christ.

Lastly, further areas need to be dealt with, to build on this foundation. Examples of such areas are the client's concept of God, forgiveness, parenting skills, eating habits, victory over temptation, communication skills, work habits or finding God's will.

The Exchanged Life is simply exchanging what the world says is life for what God says is life. Exchanged Life counseling is helping others to see this can be true for themselves in their situations and by faith to appropriate it.

AN INTEGRATION OF PERSONAL HISTORY AND PRESENT LIVING

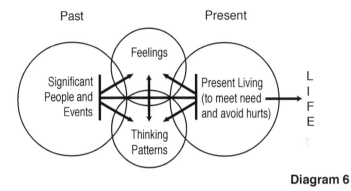

Diagram 6

A NEW IDENTITY

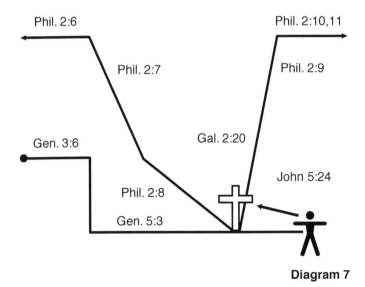

Diagram 7

Chapter five

Counseling Techniques

Exchanged Life counseling uses many techniques, most of which are not unique, except
for the consistent use of visual aids.

Counseling Techniques

Exchanged Life counseling is counseling. Therefore, basic counseling skills that are generally used in counseling are also used in Exchanged Life counseling. These are also referred to as communication skills. We will here consider eleven of these skills as the first area of the techniques used in Exchanged Life counseling to be considered.

The counselor needs to be prepared. To enter a counseling framework suddenly, with no preparation, greatly reduces the effectiveness of what can take place. In the best of circumstances the counselor prepares himself by praying for himself and the client, by reviewing what has taken place in previous interviews, and by relaxing and clearing his thinking. The place is prepared to remove distractions and to facilitate work. In an office, this can be done with comfortable furnishings and accessories. In a public place, it is best to have the client face the counselor and away from other people.

To pay attention so that the client knows he is being listened to, the counselor can do several physical things. The counselor can face the client squarely with an open posture, lean toward the client and maintain good eye contact. This physical posture can be very intense so the counselor should seek to be relaxed. These simple skills help the counselor to pay attention and communicate this to the client.

One of the most critical of these communication skills is listening. Most people are not very good listeners. Hearing is a natural ability that we don't have to think about to use. But, listening is an art that needs to be learned. The counselor listening carefully will be listening to the content and feelings expressed by the client. This involves listening to the words, the energy level and the paralinguistic clues used by the client in order to get a full picture of what is meant by what is said. Such Bible passages as Proverbs 18:13 and Job 32:11-12a show how important listening is.

Observation is another of the skills that can be developed. The nonverbal or body language will either confirm or contradict what is being said. The most important point of such observation is the face. The emotions that are going on within the person are usually demonstrated on the face. This demonstration is involuntary and very fleeting, lasting only about a tenth of a second.

Whereas attending, listening and observing pervade the entire counseling process, there are other skills that fit best at definite times. During the early part of the counseling process skills like concreteness, respect and empathy are appropriate. Later on in the process skills like confrontation, self-disclosure and immediacy fit the best.

During the early part of counseling the emphasis is on learning and understanding. The client needs to be as concrete or specific as possible in order to understand clearly. If the client states what is happening in generalities it makes it very difficult for the counselor to understand. To help become more specific the counselor can ask questions like: "How do you know?" "What do you mean?" "Could you give me an example?" Being concrete can help avoid major mistakes in understanding.

Respect is something every person wants. Respect recognizes the uniqueness and dignity of each person. The counselor can learn to accept and deal with each individual as an individual. The temptation can be there to group people together into categories and deal with them in that way. To "pigeon hole" is easy, but it does not show respect. Respect recognizes the individual is an individual and shows itself in the way the individual is treated.

At times a counselor may feel that being a counselor is an exalted position. In Exchanged Life counseling, it is especially necessary that the counselor be genuine. It is wrong to hide behind some role or to play a part. The counselor must counsel from life not from a text book. This means being genuine is of utmost importance.

The Exchanged Life counselor knows the difference between sympathy and empathy. Sympathy is an older word that means to feel together with another person. It carries the idea of knowing where a person is and being right there with them. The sympathetic counselor may become so involved that he is unable to help. Empathy is a more recent word and is slightly different. In empathy the counselor knows where the client is but is not there in the midst of the problem with him. The empathic counselor remains outside the problem in order to help.

There are times when the counselor needs to confront clients about themselves or what they are doing. Confrontation is a powerful skill that can be either tremendously helpful or devastating to the client. The absolute requirement for effective confrontation is that it must be done in love. If it is not done in love, it is judgmental and damaging. Along with an attitude of love, the best confrontation is tentative in its use and leads the client to confront himself. One form of confrontation is called immediacy. This is when the counselor must bring to the attention of the client something that is taking place between them in the counseling session. Immediacy can be simply stated as dealing with you and me, here and now.

A helpful counseling skill that the Exchanged Life counselor uses is hat of self-disclosure. There are times when the counselor tells the client about himself. This enables the client to understand that what the counselor is sharing is real life not only theory. The counselor counsels from his own life showing the reality of the indwelling Christ. Since the counselor has not become perfect in all areas of life, the telling of personal growth can give hope to the client. When using self-disclosure the counselor must stick close to two rules. first, be very, brief. Second, know clearly why any personal material is shared. Along with counseling skills another technique used in Exchanged Life counseling is the use of visual aids. Often a white board, news print, chalk board or note pad is used to draw out the ideas being discussed. This is always done in a highly personal way and never in an abstract unrelated-to-life way. The most notable use of visual aids is the use of charts or diagrams to show and explain the Exchanged Life. These diagrams are used to illustrate what is taking place in the client's life. They are also used to teach foundational truth for spiritual growth and how that can relate to what is happening. The use of such charts can be very effective, if a canned memorized approach is studiously avoided.

The spiritual resources expected in any Christian counseling are definitely used in Exchanged Life counseling. Prayer is an integral part of counseling. The counselor needs prayer and the client needs prayer. The counselor needs to pray and the client needs to pray. The reading of and meditating on the Bible is a constant factor. The Bible is never used to "badger" people. It is used to help where it fits the best into the client's life situation. Specific passages from the Bible must be used carefully as they are applied to the life of the client in a very personal way.

Homework is a technique that is used almost with every counseling session. The type of homework depends on the person and on what is taking place. The homework assignment may involve reading a booklet or part of a book. It may be listening to an audio tape or carrying out some activity. The major part of the homework assignments revolves around the reading, studying and meditating on the Bible. Because the counseling approach of Exchanged Life counseling is from the spiritual aspect of life, the Bible is extremely important as a homework assignment.

There are other techniques that may be used in Exchanged Life counseling. These will greatly vary from counselor to counselor because they depend on a variety of factors. If available, the counselor may have the client watch certain video tapes that relate to what is needed. The counselor may use the testimony of a previous client if given permission to do so. Various psychological instruments may be used to more quickly understand the client. These and other techniques may be used in Exchanged Life counseling to aid the client in the most effective way available.

Exchanged Life counseling uses many techniques in counseling. Most are not unique. The most unique is the use of charts or diagrams. These are only visual aids to help make truths clearer. Because they are tools, the counselor is free to use them in the way that is best for the client. They must also be used in a way that best fits the person of the counselor.

The following set of visual aids have been adapted over the past twenty-five years. The ideas for them have come from many people. Some of those I can remember and want to give credit to are: Neil Anderson, Donald Gray Barnhouse, Ray Burwick, DeVern Fromke, Bill Gillham, Paul Kaschel, L. E. Maxwell, Ruth Paxson, Bob Smith, and Charles Solomon.

POSITION OF MANKIND

1. The first person

SIN and SATAN

1. Open fellowship with God.

2. Total dependence on God.

3. Identity found in the Lord.

4. Free service for the Lord.

2. Fallen people

SIN and SATAN

1. Separated from God, no fellowship with God.

2. Illusion of independence.

3. Identity found in self.

4. Slave to sin, and can't change.

3. Regenerated people

SIN and SATAN

1. New intimate fellowship with God.

2. Free choice to live dependent.

3. Christ identity possible.

4. Bondage to sin broken, free to choose.

Diagram 8

THE MODEL OF HUMAN MAKEUP
TAKEN FROM THE TEMPLE

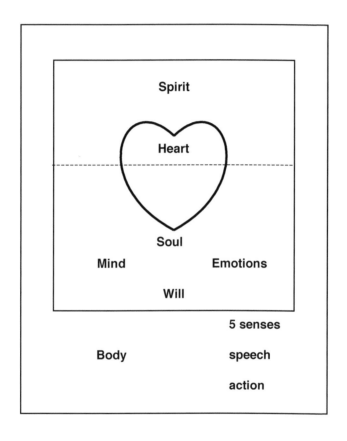

Diagram 9

RESULTS OF SIN AND SALVATION

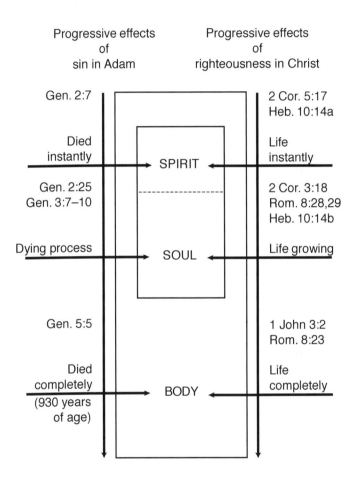

Progressive effects of sin in Adam		Progressive effects of righteousness in Christ
Gen. 2:7		2 Cor. 5:17 Heb. 10:14a
Died instantly	→ SPIRIT ←	Life instantly
Gen. 2:25 Gen. 3:7–10		2 Cor. 3:18 Rom. 8:28,29 Heb. 10:14b
Dying process	→ SOUL ←	Life growing
Gen. 5:5		1 John 3:2 Rom. 8:23
Died completely (930 years of age)	→ BODY ←	Life completely

Salvation in the same way as sin totally affects the entire person.

Diagram 10

THE UNREGENERATE PERSON

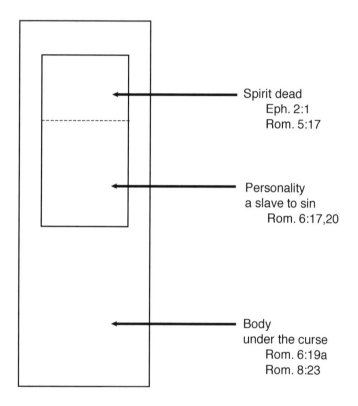

Spirit dead
Eph. 2:1
Rom. 5:17

Personality
a slave to sin
Rom. 6:17,20

Body
under the curse
Rom. 6:19a
Rom. 8:23

Diagram 11

THE REGENERATED PERSON

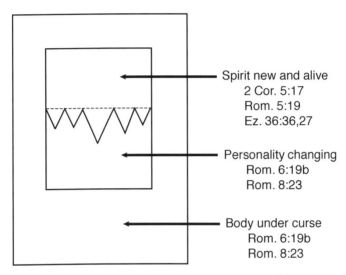

Spirit new and alive
2 Cor. 5:17
Rom. 5:19
Ez. 36:36,27

Personality changing
Rom. 6:19b
Rom. 8:23

Body under curse
Rom. 6:19b
Rom. 8:23

Diagram 12

FLESHLY CHRISTIAN

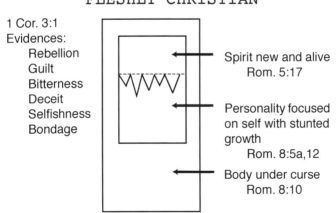

1 Cor. 3:1
Evidences:
  Rebellion
  Guilt
  Bitterness
  Deceit
  Selfishness
  Bondage

Spirit new and alive
Rom. 5:17

Personality focused
on self with stunted
growth
Rom. 8:5a,12

Body under curse
Rom. 8:10

Diagram 13

SPIRITUAL CHRISTIAN

Gal. 5:16,18; 6:1

Evidences:
   Submission
   Forgiveness
   Love
   Truth
   God's will
   Strength

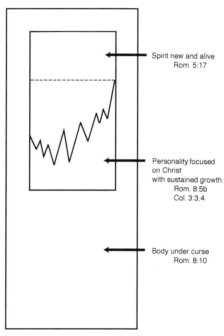

Spirit new and alive
Rom. 5:17

Personality focused
on Christ
with sustained growth
Rom. 8:5b
Col. 3:3,4

Body under curse
Rom. 8:10

Diagram 14

CHRIST'S LIFE

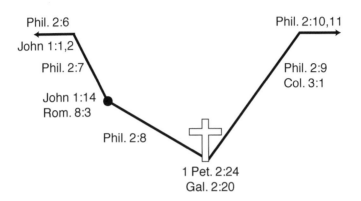

Phil. 2:6
John 1:1,2
Phil. 2:7
John 1:14
Rom. 8:3
Phil. 2:8

Phil. 2:10,11
Phil. 2:9
Col. 3:1

1 Pet. 2:24
Gal. 2:20

Diagram 15

LIFE IN ADAM

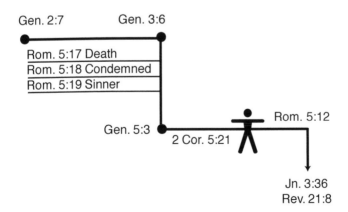

Gen. 2:7   Gen. 3:6
Rom. 5:17 Death
Rom. 5:18 Condemned
Rom. 5:19 Sinner

Gen. 5:3
2 Cor. 5:21

Rom. 5:12

Jn. 3:36
Rev. 21:8

Diagram 16

LIFE IN CHRIST

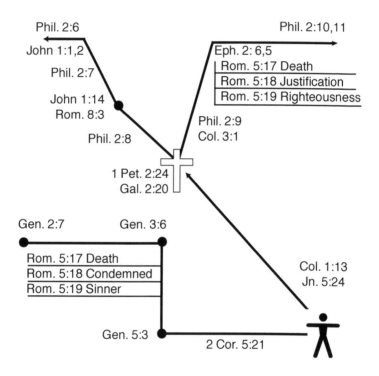

Phil. 2:6
John 1:1,2
Phil. 2:7
John 1:14
Rom. 8:3
Phil. 2:8

Phil. 2:10,11
Eph. 2: 6,5
Rom. 5:17 Death
Rom. 5:18 Justification
Rom. 5:19 Righteousness
Phil. 2:9
Col. 3:1

1 Pet. 2:24
Gal. 2:20

Gen. 2:7   Gen. 3:6

Rom. 5:17 Death
Rom. 5:18 Condemned
Rom. 5:19 Sinner

Col. 1:13
Jn. 5:24

Gen. 5:3
2 Cor. 5:21

Diagram 17

Chapter Six

The Goal of Counseling

The overall goal of Exchanged Life counseling is to aid in spiritual maturity to such an extent that spiritual truth becomes experiential reality.

The Goal of Counseling

What is the purpose of counseling? Why should a person seek counseling? What does the counselor seek to accomplish? These are the kinds of questions that reveal the goal of counseling. All counselors have in mind what they would like to see happen as a result of the time spent with the client. The reaching of this goal is the basis for determining if the counseling is successful or not. For instance, if the counselor's goal is that the client continue to come for counseling, success is determined by how long that client continues in counseling.

In order to clarify the goal of Exchanged Life counseling, it will help to consider first some common goals for counseling. Often counselors are seeking to aid the client to be able to cope more effectively with life. Many methods can be used for discovering ineffective methods of coping and then replacing them with more effective ones. Therefore, if the client is better able to cope with the pressures of life, the counseling is successful. The goal has been reached.

Another common expectation is to make life more comfortable. The client faces difficulties, and these difficulties are making life uncomfortable. The counselor then will seek to aid the client to set goals for life which can be reached and will make life more comfortable. Success can then be measured by how well the client is able to reach the goals that have been chosen to make life more comfortable. This kind of goal for counseling may come from the client rather than the counselor.

A very common goal that clients often have in seeking counseling is to change other people or change circumstances. There are conflicts at home, conflicts at work or conflicts at church. How can these conflicts be resolved? One way is to change jobs or change churches or even change families. Counselors and/or clients may look at changing situations as the best way to deal with the pressures of life. When such changes do take place the counseling is determined to be successful.

These kinds of goals in counseling rely upon the resources of the individual to be able to handle life's stresses in a more effective way. Depending on the value system of the counselor all or some of the previously mentioned goals could be used. If one is focused on the individual's resources as the only or primary resource which can be tapped into for change, the above stated goals, or others like them, are good goals for counseling.

When counseling focuses on the spiritual aspect of life as being of major importance, there must be a different goal. The Exchanged Life counselor approaches counseling with the conviction that the spiritual dimension of life is the most important. The result is that the goal of counseling is different from usual goals.

The overall goal of Exchanged Life counseling is that the client will come to understand his identity in Christ and begin to experience it in the vicissitudes of his life. The reason for this goal is that the resources for change come from the Lord. The exchanging of a self-centered life lived out of ones own resources for a Christ-centered life lived out of the Lord's resources is the basis for deep, long lasting change. Another way to state this is, the believer's identification or union with Christ in His death, burial, resurrection, ascension and seating at the right hand of the Father is the foundation for change.

This overall goal can be broken down into more specific aspects. The first is to aid the client to understand and grow in Christ-likeness (Romans 8:28,29; 2 Corinthians 3:18). God is at work in all things for the client's good which is to conform him to the likeness of Christ. The Exchanged Life counselor seeks to be an instrument in the hands of the Lord to aid in the client in the process of being transformed into the likeness of Christ.

A second aspect of the overall goal is called spiritual maturity (Ephesians 4:13; 2 Peter 3:18). God gave to the church gifted leaders to assist believers in becoming mature or attaining the whole measure of the fullness of Christ. Exchanged Life counseling is clearly pastoral in seeking to aid clients to grow in grace and in the knowledge of Christ, thus growing in spiritual maturity.

Seeing the fruit of the Spirit start to be consistently shown in a believer's life is a third aspect of the overall goal (Galatians 5:22,23). Character that is growing in Christ-likeness will be evidencing more and more love, joy, peace, patience, kindness, goodness, gentleness and self-control. The Exchanged Life counselor seeks to aid the client to see where the acts of the flesh are evident and begin to see them replaced by the fruit of the Spirit. As the client appropriates his identity in Christ, this change takes place.

The fourth and final aspect of the overall goal is freedom in Christ's life (2 Corinthians 3:17; Galatians 5:1,13). To know the truth which is Christ, is to be set free from the law of sin and death, for where the Spirit of the Lord is there is freedom. This freedom in Christ is not to be used to indulge the flesh but is to be used to serve others in love. The Exchanged Life counselor seeks to aid the client to grasp and begin to live in the freedom found in Christ rather than to continue in bondage to sin.

The Exchanged Life counselor seeks to keep the spiritual aspect of life the most importance. The goal is to see spiritual truth become an experiential reality in the life of the client. When this takes place, many if not most of the problems the client faces change or begin to change or the client begins to see Christ's sufficiency to live with them. **Through exchanging a self-centered way of life for a Christ-centered one (i.e. an Exchanged Life) the client begins to realize the experiential reality of the cross and resurrection life.**

Chapter Seven

Theological Constructs and Terms

The Exchanged Life is the exchange of a self-centered life lived out of the Christian's own resources, as if he were still in Adam, for a Christ-centered life lived out of Christ's resources because he is in Christ.

Theological Constructs and Terms

Because Exchanged Life counseling focuses on the spiritual area of life, theology is an essential subject. Of the nine major divisions of theology, three will be focused on because of their relation to Exchanged Life counseling. These three divisions are: the doctrine of the Bible, the doctrine of man and sin, and the doctrine of salvation. These different divisions will not be examined thoroughly. They will be examined only in those areas that are germane to the subject at hand.

The first of the three areas is the doctrine of the Bible. This is foremost because the Bible is the source of authority in the ministry of Exchanged Life counseling. The Bible is superior to any other source of information, in practice as well as theory. Therefore, there are two key areas to note about the Bible: the first is the view of the Bible itself, the second is the use of the Bible.

The Bible is God's Word. A short statement of such belief could say: "We believe in the plenary and verbal inspiration of the inerrant and infallible Bible, both old and new testaments, a perfect, final authority." This statement gives the Bible a high place in what is to be believed in Exchanged Life counseling. The Bible is the final authority—not the counselor, not the method, not the ministry, not the client, only the Bible.

The high view of the Bible must not remain only a belief but must be related to what is taking place. A counselor may say that he maintains such a high view of the Bible, but how he handles the Bible reveals what he really believes. In Exchanged Life counseling, the Bible is the supreme guide. Everything must be measured by the Bible. The Bible and psychology are not two different but equal authorities that can be integrated to form a counseling method. The Bible sets forth God's truth, and psychology must be evaluated by it. Exchanged Life counseling approaches the Bible as the final source of authority. Psychology is very helpful in understanding people but must be evaluated by the Bible. The use of the Bible reflects the view held of the Bible. Exchanged Life counseling seeks to start from, move with and reach conclusions by the Bible. Not having a complete understanding will lead to missing this standard, but that does not change the standard.

The second area that directly relates to Exchanged Life counseling is the doctrine of man and sin. The Biblical model of man was dealt with in an earlier section. A concise statement in this area that shows this truth clearly could say: "We believe in the creation of mankind by God in His own image and likeness, and out of the dust of the earth. This creation results in man being both material and immaterial consisting of spirit, soul and body. We believe in the fall of all mankind in Adam and the universal total depravity of the human race resulting in the guilt and lost condition of all men everywhere outside of Christ."

Man is a spiritual being having a unique personality (i.e. soul) and physique (i.e. body). God always deals with the person as a whole person rather than with only one of the aspects of his makeup. The unregenerate human spirit is called the "old man" which at salvation is exchanged for the "new man." What happened at the fall of mankind into sin begins to be reversed at salvation. The flesh which is often referred to as the sinful nature is not removed at salvation because it is not a part of a person's makeup but a way of living.

The question must be raised about the definition of sin. Sin is primarily a lack of conformity to the character and will of God. This may be general or specific, known or unknown, voluntary or involuntary. There are a multitude of results that flow from sin, such as meaninglessness, depression or loneliness; but these are results and not in themselves sin.

Because of the fall, sin has been given a position of being the legal ruler over mankind. The Christian has been set free from this rulership. Yet the Christian may still choose to live under sin's rule even though he has been set free. Because sin has permeated every area of man's life, the propensity to sin is strong. This is why sin can be spoken of as having power as though it were an entity in itself which it is not. The Exchanged Life counselor recognizes sin and sin's results, dealing with each in an appropriate way.

The last of the three areas is the doctrine of salvation. A clear statement could say: "We believe in the absolute necessity of salvation by grace through personal faith in the substitutionary death of Jesus Christ, resulting in all true believers thus saved being kept saved forever. We believe in the believer being able to live the Christian life in the present through appropriation of the Exchanged Life." To amplify this last sentence a further statement needs to be made, "We believe that the Christian partakes of eternal life (Christ's life) at the time of new birth, that identification with Christ in His crucifixion, burial, resurrection and ascension brought the death of the "old man" and the life of the "new man." This may become a revealed experiential reality through a decision to lose one's life (total surrender) and to appropriate the Christ-life by faith. It is continuously revealed by abiding in the Spirit and pursuing holiness. Victorious living is Christ living His life through the believer by the believer's faith and obedience under the Holy Spirit. This does not teach passivity, sinless perfection or the deification of man."

Exchanged Life counseling seeks to recognize and build on what took place at salvation. This statement in itself points out that the first step in Exchanged Life counseling is salvation. Everything else is built on this foundation. These are great facts that became true at the moment a person becomes a Christian. At salvation a person is justified. He is declared righteous on the basis of the work of Christ on the cross. Christ died for man's sins so that forgiveness might be realized.

Not only did Christ die for the Christian to provide forgiveness and justification, but the Christian also died with Christ to provide life and victory. These may or may not be seen in the daily living of the Christian but they are true nonetheless because God said they are true. These great truths related to salvation may remain just truths and have no relationship to life. This need not be the case. What is true can be appropriated for daily living.

Spiritual growth is often hindered by the great enemies of the Christian–the world, the flesh and the devil. Exchanged Life counseling touches on the world and devil but focuses on the flesh. Scripture teaches that the flesh is not a part of a person's makeup but is a person's way of living. Salvation changes the person but not all the ways that person lives which are still in the process of changing.

Exchanged Life counseling is focused on the true spiritual identity of the Christian. By coming to understand this and living out of it the Christian's life can begin to change. This change may be dramatic or it may be gradual. Either way the choice for growth has been made through the decision the Christian has made to appropriate his union with Christ.

At this point we need to stop and restate what has been said in a different way. There is the need to be specific in the use of theological terms and in the use of Scriptural evidence.

The Bible is the plenary verbally inspired, inerrant, infallible Word of God which results in it being God's authoritative revelation of His will and truth to mankind. The Bible is the final authority in all matters of faith and practice (2 Peter 1:20, 21; 2 Timothy 3:16; 1 Corinthians 10:11; Matthew 5:17, 18; Luke 24:25; John 10:35; Mark 12:36; Zechariah 7:12).

Mankind was created innocent but yielded to temptation and became a sinner (Genesis 3:1-7; Romans 5:12, 14). The whole human race is organically united to its natural head Adam (Acts 17:26; Romans 5:12; 1 Corinthians 15:22). All men are born in Adam, condemned, sinful, and unable to please God

(Romans 3:10-20; 5:12-14; 1 King 8:46; 1 John 1:8-10; 2 Timothy 3:2-4; Titus 1:15). Sin is any lack of conformity to the character of and law of God, either in act, disposition or state (Galatians 3:10; James 2:10; 1 John 3:4). Sin results in Judgment and spiritual death (John 3:18; Romans 5:15-18; Ephesians 4:18).

Justification is that judicial act of God whereby the sinner is declared righteous on the basis of the righteousness of Christ (Romans 3:21-30; Galatians 2:15-21). This forensic act includes remission of sins (Romans 4:5-8; Acts 13:38, 39) and the imputation of Christ's righteousness (2 Corinthians 5:21; Romans 5:17; Philippians 3:8,9). The source of justification is the grace of God (Romans 3:24), the basis of justification is the death of Jesus Christ (Romans 5:9), and the condition of justification is faith (Romans 5:1).

The people justified by God are secured by God so that they can never completely fall from the state of grace and fail. These individuals will persevere until salvation is completed (Philippians 1:6; Romans 8:38,39; John 10:27-29; Romans 11:29).

Regeneration and conversion deal more with the changes in the person than in the changes in status. Regeneration is the implanting of the principle of new life in those who are saved (John 10:10; 1 John 5:11,12; 2 Corinthians 5:17; Ezekiel 36:26, 27), which results in the process of changing man's disposition intellectually, emotionally, and morally (Ephesians 2:10; 4:23,24).

Conversion is that act of God whereby He causes the individual to turn to Himself in repentance and faith, and consequently the resulting conscious act of the individual whereby he turns to God in repentance and faith (2 Chronicles 33:12,13; Luke 19:8,9; Acts 16:33). Conversion involves both repentance: a change of view, feeling, and purpose in regards to sin (Romans 4:2; Psalm 51:2,10,14; Titus 3:4-8), and faith: a working of the Holy Spirit whereby man is convinced of the truth of the gospel and places his trust in the promises of God in Christ (Romans 3:25,26; Galatians 2:16; Ephesians 2:8).

The result of salvation is sanctification. Sanctification is both the positional and progressive work of the Holy Spirit (1 Corinthians 6:11; Hebrews 10:14; Acts 20:32). It is a fact at salvation (Romans 6:6; Colossians 3:9). All that is true of a Christian became true at salvation when he was taken out of Adam and placed in Christ (1 Corinthians 15:22; John 3:1-21). The process of the outworking of salvation (Philippians 2:12, 13) is the renewal of the moral image of God in man (2 Corinthians 3:18; Romans 8:29) enabling good works to be done (Ephesians 2:8-10; Galatians 2:19; Romans 6:11-13). The process of sanctification consummates in glorification when the whole person has been affected (1 John 3:2; Philippians 3:20,21; Romans 8:22-25).

Since theology is a key ingredient in Exchanged Life counseling, there will be different approaches because of differences in theology. The theology which is expressed in these pages is in agreement with most evangelical Bible teaching churches. It is a mistake to put all the varieties of Exchanged Life counseling into one lump. There are those who are from the various positions of evangelical theology who take the truth of the Bible very seriously in ministering to hurting people. Their specific theology greatly affects the outworking of their ministry. The truth of the believer's identification with Christ will be applied in various ways.

The terms used in Exchanged Life counseling can be misleading unless they are clearly defined. There are several key terms that must be clearly understood to avoid much of the confusion which prevails.

Identification is an often used word in Exchanged Life counseling. It simply means to identify or to unite together with another so as to have one common interest or purpose. The Christian is identified with Christ. This takes place at salvation but is often not realized in experience until a later time. Exchanged Life counseling seeks to aid the Christian to see the reality of this truth in his daily living. When the Christian lives the same as the world system that Christian is not living out his real identity but is living out a former identity in Adam.

At salvation the process takes place that changes identity. This process is crucifixion or death which leads to new resurrection life. Death does not mean to annihilate. If it did, Jesus would have ceased to exist when He was put to death. Death is the lack of life, just like darkness is the lack of light. Key results of death are separation and a change of relationship. The Christian died with Christ and the result is being separated from the rule of sin and having a new relationship to it. The opposite is also true. The Christian died with Christ and the result is being separated unto the Lord and having a new relationship with Him.

The question is, "What died?" The Bible is clear that the "old man" is what died. What then is the "old man"? Broadly the "old man" is what the Christian was before being saved. Specifically the "old man" is the unregenerated human spirit. Spiritually the Christian died with Christ and was resurrected with Christ a "new man" i.e. a regenerated human spirit. Through death and resurrection the Christian becomes a new creation; the old has gone, and the new has come.

Since the "old man" has been replaced with the "new man" the conclusion could be that the Christian is now made new. This is true spiritually but not true psychologically or physically. flesh is a continuing problem. flesh is a common word in the New Testament. It is used in many ways. flesh is not an entity but a condition or way of living learned before salvation and taught by the world. After salvation, fleshly living patterns are a continuing problem that will not be changed totally until the Lord returns or the Christian goes to be with Him.

Sin, like flesh, is not an entity but an action. To understand how we sin, sin can be portrayed as a person. This does not make it a person or entity. Sin is always activity, or the result of that activity, corrupting the individual. Adam's sin resulted in corrupting the whole human race so that all people are sinners and act it out in their own way. Sin can't be blamed for what takes place because sin is the individual acting in certain ways. Paul in Romans 7 speaks of sin as a person to help understand how strong that propensity is. In doing so he is using a common literary device to help understand and not teaching that sin is an entity in itself. The propensity to sin and to live after the fleshly patterns are extremely close. They are so close that they are often referred to as the sinful nature. Exchanged Life counselors may use this term but usually don't because it is so often used incorrectly. For instance, the old man is not a part of the sinful nature. It is often indiscriminately stated as though it were, which creates confusion and misunderstanding.

Putting these terms together will help to see Exchanged Life counseling in a clear light. The Christian's identity is changed from "in Adam" to "in Christ" at salvation. The "old man" was changed to a "new man." The fleshly living patterns, however, have not been changed so that the Christian can live as though he were still in Adam. Living as though in Adam does not fit the reality of being in Christ and, therefore, creates many difficulties. The Exchanged Life counselor seeks to aid the Christian to realize and appropriate his true identity. When this starts, changes take place. These changes can continue as the Christian continues to live on the basis of who he really is in Christ.

Many Christians have not come to know who they really are in Christ. The Lord then will work through their situations to bring them to the end of their own resources. When the Christian is broken of self-will so that it is no longer I but Christ, he begins to live out of his true identity and begins to find victory over the power of his propensity to sin. This growth takes a lifetime culminating when the Lord either takes him home through death or in the second coming.

The Exchanged Life is the exchange of a self-centered life lived out of one's own resources for a Christ-centered life lived out of His resources.